David A. Hansen, Architect

RESHAPING CORPORATE CULTURE

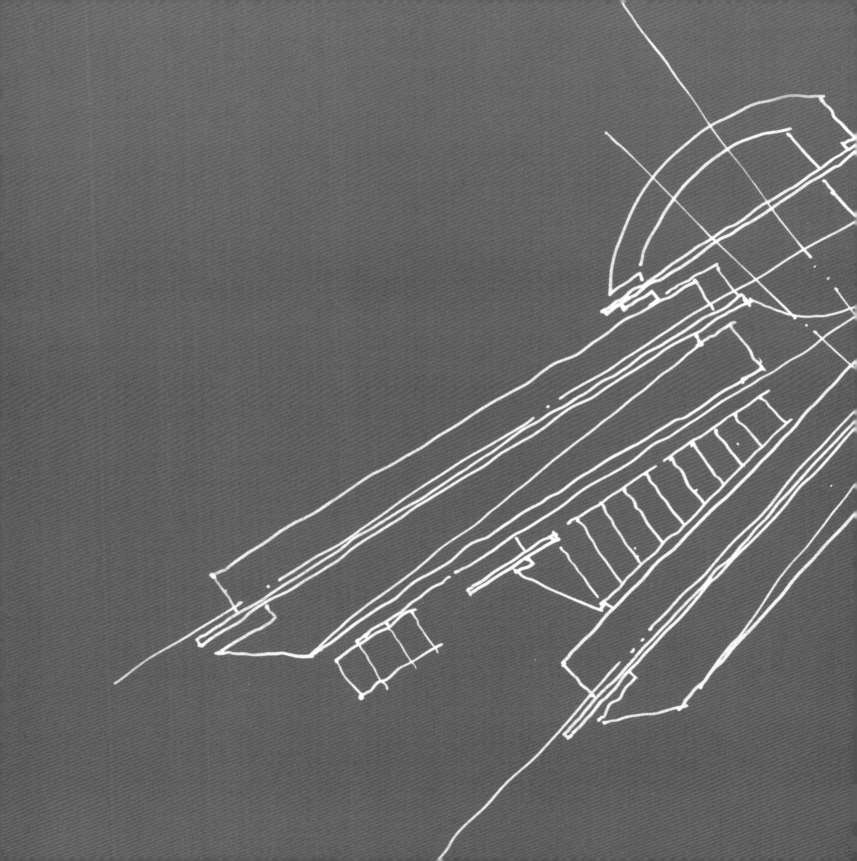

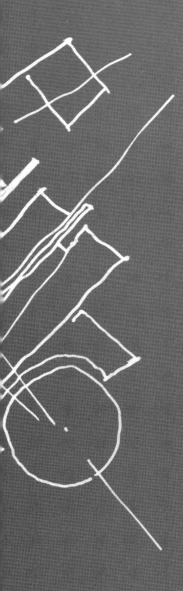

David A. Hansen, Architect

RESHAPING CORPORATE CULTURE

images
Publishing

Published in Australia in 2005 by
The Images Publishing Group Pty Ltd
ABN 89 059 734 431
6 Bastow Place, Mulgrave, Victoria 3170, Australia
Tel: +61 3 9561 5544 Fax: +61 3 9561 4860
books@images.com.au
www.imagespublishing.com

Copyright © The Images Publishing Group Pty Ltd 2005
The Images Publishing Group Reference Number: 630

National Library of Australia
Cataloguing-in-Publication entry:

David A. Hansen: reshaping corporate culture.

ISBN 1 86470 126 9.

1. Hansen, David A. 2. Perkins & Will – Employees. 3. Architects – United
States. 4. Architecture, Modern – 20th century – United States.

720.920973

Coordinating editor: Robyn Beaver

Designed by The Graphic Image Studio Pty Ltd, Mulgrave, Australia
www.tgis.com.au

Digital production and print by Everbest Printing Co. Ltd. in Hong Kong/China

IMAGES has included on its website a page for special notices in relation to
this and our other publications. Please visit www.imagespublishing.com.

Contents

Built Projects

On the Boards

Appendix

Preface

By David Hansen

David Hansen

I have always had a profound interest in the issues of site, context, environment and materiality that float about the peripheries of all design projects. While these parameters are always at play, the act of listening to clients is paramount.

In architecture, and especially in the design of corporate and commercial complexes, I have found that complete immersion into the culture and vision of the organization, listening and observing specific strategic goals, yields a point of view and focus that generates uncommon solutions. Because of this awareness, I have never felt a personal or stylistic signature to my buildings was either necessary or appropriate. For me, the act of weighing diverse factors and interpreting them through a personal filter enhances the development of an ultimate form that expresses those conditions and demands for a specific solution for a specific client.

Since joining the practice of Perkins+Will in 1986, I have had the opportunity to master plan more than 40 million square feet of facilities and design more than 18 million square feet of corporate and mixed-use facilities worldwide. The projects selected for this volume illustrate my theory on the effect architecture has on defining the culture and values of a corporation—a

BUILT PROJECTS

W.W. Grainger, Inc. Headquarters
Lake Forest, Illinois

In 1927, when William W. Grainger founded W.W. Grainger, Inc. (Grainger) he had a simple mission: to offer his growing population of industrial customers convenient access to a large supply of electric motors. Seventy-seven years later, the company's mission remains the same. Grainger is in the business of keeping business in business. The MotorBook, as it was originally called, is the basis for the current Grainger catalog that has since expanded to more than 500,000 supplies and 2.5 million repair parts—with "service" as the byword. Grainger leadership credits much of its longstanding success to the company's ability to be flexible and adapt to changing customer, employee and shareholder values.

When Grainger leadership approached David Hansen of Perkins+Will to lead a team in the design of its corporate campus headquarters complex, 30 miles north of Chicago, in Lake Forest, Illinois, the goal for the project was also simple: create a phased campus facility based on principles of flexibility, connectivity and responsiveness to the customer, the employees and the community. Since this new corporate campus represents the first time in its 75-year history that all Grainger corporate officers will locate in one central location, leadership was looking forward to an opportunity to use the campus as a way to align its physical facilities with its corporate culture.

12

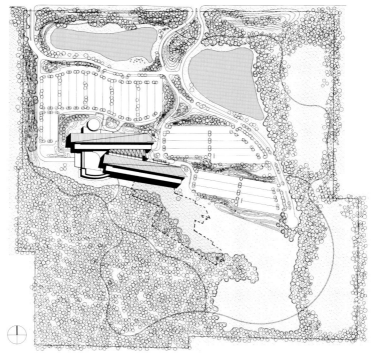

Site plan

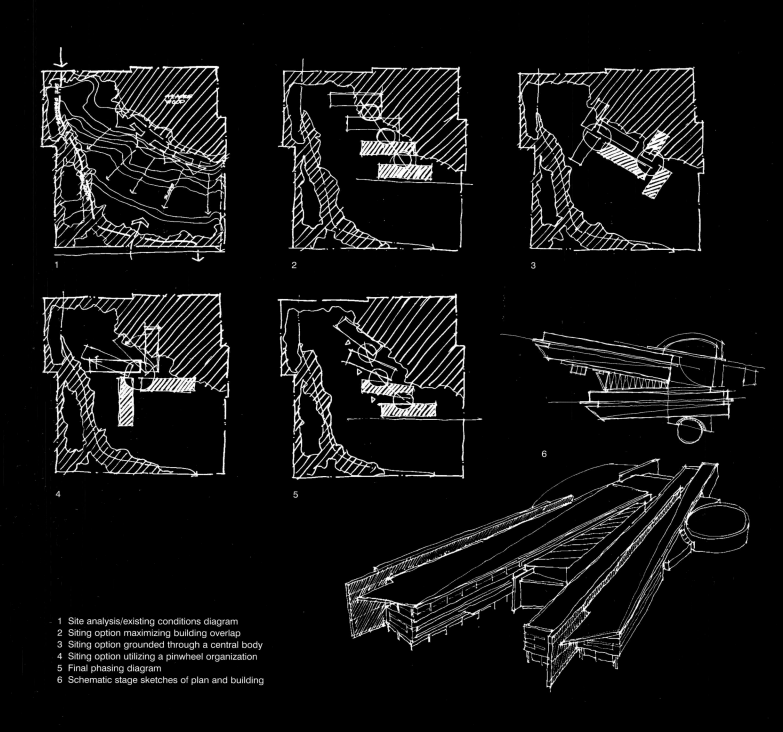

14

1 Site analysis/existing conditions diagram
2 Siting option maximizing building overlap
3 Siting option grounded through a central body
4 Siting option utilizing a pinwheel organization
5 Final phasing diagram
6 Schematic stage sketches of plan and building

W.W. Grainger, Inc. Headquarters

Flexibility, connectivity and responsiveness—the spirit behind the planning strategy—drove all design and client team decisions from project inception to completion. The first phase, completed in 1999, is an 800,000-square-foot structure made up of two elongated rectangular office wings linked by a fan-shaped central atrium. Hansen's team implemented a master plan for the site that mapped out alternate future scenarios for Grainger, ranging from maintaining the original complex to a build-out that nearly doubles the building area.

In response to the client's requirement for a flexible interior environment, the team realized a planning strategy for Grainger's large interrelated departments and their changing needs, comprised of two paired building wings, each 630 feet by 120 feet. A 50-foot clear span structural system is based on possible planning modules and establishes an open column-free environment, freeing up the interior space to maximize flexibility.

The atrium becomes the central point of vitality, the area of connectivity within the campus, with bridges linking the separate building wings from both sides of the complex. Hansen located all support facilities and amenities in close proximity to the atrium, including the food service area, a wellness and fitness center, visitors' center, and a conference/employee development center with a 500-seat auditorium. The sunlit atrium is the heart of the complex and is designed to encourage interface, conversation, casual and formal meetings and promote and elevate the enjoyment of staff interaction.

Grainger's commitment to being responsive to the community set a standard for the campus structure that visually connects the building to the site. The team achieved this by developing a strategy that conserves the 42 acres of woodlands and wetlands. Wanting to also establish a "good neighbor" policy, extensive berms and landscaping on the major frontage of the site spared

W.W. Grainger, Inc. Headquarters

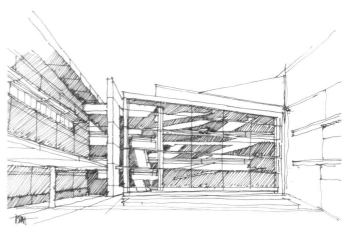

any visual intrusion into the neighboring residential areas. The exterior of the building is clad in earth-toned hues of Venetian Gold granite and Villebois limestone that blend into the landscape's earthy hues.

Hansen and his team designed the three- and four-story buildings with a recessed base and top floor, thereby reducing the mass of the complex. Large projected eaves and linear projected screening elements above windows act as solar shading elements, reducing the interior thermal load of the building. To further reduce energy consumption, all cooling requirements for the building are supplied by means of an internal ice storage system.

According to Grainger's Vice-President of Administrative Services, Michael Murray, the campus headquarters building has met its objective of expressing the continuing vision of William W. Grainger: a culture that conveys a new vision and respect for the community, employees and their work environment. He states, "David's guidance and concern for the total workplace environment created an office workplace that has resulted in achieving our organizational goals in recruitment, employee productivity, retention and our ability to change and grow with our customers."

17

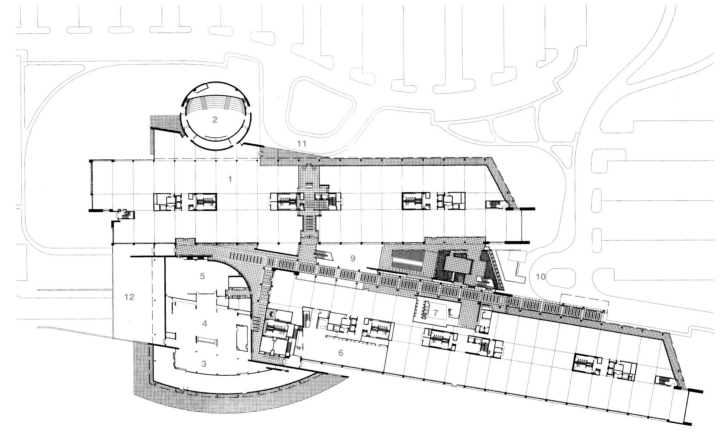

1 Typical office
2 500-seat auditorium
3 Dining
4 Servery

5 Kitchen
6 Fitness
7 Hospitality suite
8 Atrium

9 Open to below
10 Main entrance canopy
11 Auditorium drop off
12 Service and receiving

W.W. Grainger, Inc. Headquarters

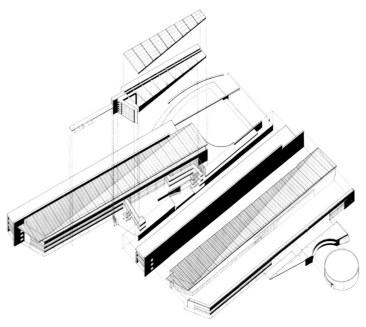

W.W. Grainger, Inc. Headquarters

"David's guidance and concern for the total workplace environment created an office workplace that has resulted in achieving our organizational goals in recruitment, employee productivity, retention and our ability to change and grow with our customers."

Michael Murray,
V.P. Administration Services

Sam Yang Company Headquarters
Taejon, Korea

In 1991, as Sam Yang Company (Sam Yang) planned its relocation to the government-sponsored Dae Duck Science Technology Park in Taejon, Korea, it sought out the expertise of architect David Hansen of Perkins+Will for his world-class knowledge of state-of-the-art research and development facilities. As one of Korea's larger, more diversified corporations, Sam Yang was looking to build a facility that would showcase its premier position in research and applied technology while maintaining a respect for the traditional aspects of Korean culture and heritage. For Sam Yang, the architectural statement of this large-scale facility presented a unique opportunity to define a distinctive public image amid Korea's rapidly growing "Science City."

To begin, Hansen led the design team in conceiving a master plan for a three-phase development of the 15.5-acre site with the goal of minimizing disruption to the natural surroundings. Buildings were designed to respond to the rolling hills and contours of the site and positioned to save major trees and forest stations. The team researched and became familiar with the ancient Korean art of spiritual influences, called *Pungsu*, that eventually informed many of the design team's planning strategies such as placement of buildings on the site and the geometric relationships between the various building structures.

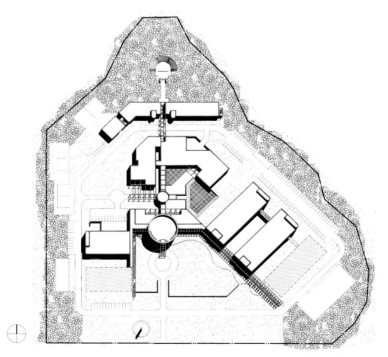

Site plan

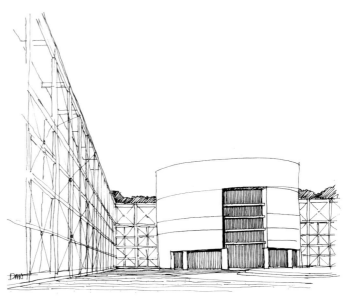

A large three-story rotunda announces the entrance into the research facility and functions as a reception hall for visitors and employees. It also houses Sam Yang's public spaces including administrative offices, a computer center and library and exhibition space. In addition, the rotunda acts as a separating device for Sam Yang and Sam Hill, the two distinct research facilities and pilot plants for applied research. The two research wings terminate at a point of intersection that serves as a common education center, equipped with lecture halls, classrooms, a 200-seat auditorium, library, and food service facility for 600 people.

Hansen's clarity of strategy for orientation and wayfinding unites the various divergent aspects of the facility, from a residential dorm to research labs and manufacturing facilities, into a single composite whole. A dominant structural grid is introduced at the entrance rotunda and moves throughout the campus to function as a continuous circulation spine to promote a ceremonial and sequential unfolding of all functions. Employees working in different areas of the building have opportunities to come together for impromptu meetings, dining and socializing. An internal courtyard acts as a common cultural amenity for the facility and is accessible to all users.

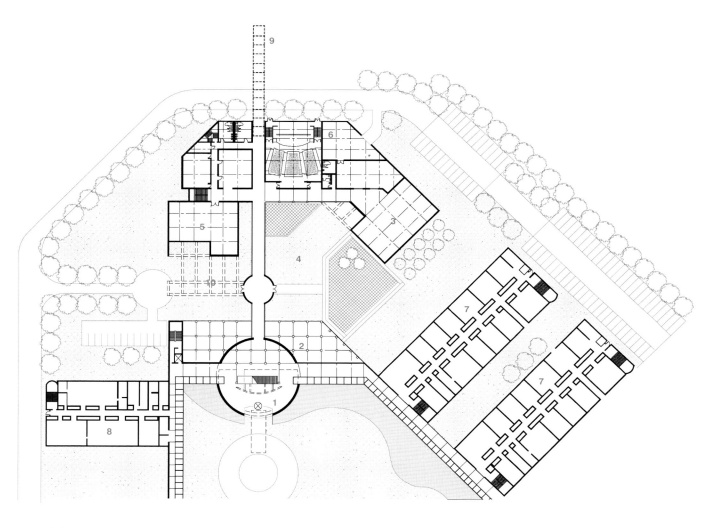

1 Lobby rotunda/main entry
2 Library/business center
3 Food service
4 Courtyard
5 Administrative offices
6 Auditorium/conference center
7 Sam Yang laboratories
8 Sam Yang laboratories
9 Bridge to residential
10 Future expansion

Sam Yang Company Headquarters

The brilliant white metal cladding and rendered concrete of the exterior stands out among the rich green landscape and surroundings. Hansen's choice of the materials was twofold: first for visual impact and second for the environmental benefit that comes from the material's reflective qualities that reduced the heat island effect on the surrounding area. A system of natural ventilation was designed for all areas of the corporate facility, except for the research laboratories. The team's extensive use of natural daylighting reduced energy use and created a comfortable workplace for the employees. Utilization of locally available construction materials also helped to reduce unnecessary cost and energy consumption that arise from the shipping of non-regional products.

Today, both the permanent and seasonally transitory employees in Sam Yang's Taejon facility have responded to the careful planning of Hansen's team by yielding greater productivity than previously enjoyed, becoming a highly interactive community with a measurable increase in the attraction and retention of researchers. The project was recently chosen by the Korean Society of Architects as its Gold medal winner in both Architecture and Cultural categories and was featured on the cover of *PLUS*, Korea's leading architectural publication.

Sears Integrated Business Headquarters

Hoffman Estates, Illinois

Few corporate relocations have stirred the emotions of the real estate community and general public as did the relocation of the Sears Integrated Business Headquarters (Sears) from the iconic Sears Tower, in the center of Chicago's business district, to a suburban corporate campus in Hoffman Estates, Illinois. At the time of the announcement, Sears laid claim to being the largest employer in the Chicago area, causing great speculation and concern about what motivated the decision.

However, when Sears approached Perkins+Will's David Hansen to design a new corporate campus for its headquarters, its goals and motivations were simple: to return to what Sears viewed as its "pre-tower" corporate culture: a much less hierarchical setting with the goal of achieving a high level of interaction, collaboration and communication. A more casual environment, the client believed, better described the values of the organization and more closely fit Sears' employee and customer values. For Sears' facilities group, a corporate campus setting not only lowered the cost of having to go outside its facility for conferencing and meeting space, but also increased communication within and between departments. This approach also gave Sears the ability to enhance effectiveness within the workplace while using its facilities as marketing and recruiting tools. In addition, Hansen's team developed planning strategies for the campus to support future expansion and compression of space requirements over the life of the buildings.

36

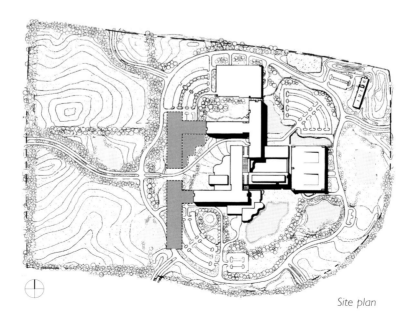

Site plan

Hansen and his design team conceived the 1,900,000-square-foot building to function as a small town, building a sense of community through the life of the town. The headquarters was therefore built as a series of five wings, varying in height from four to six stories surrounding an internal atrium, an area described as "main street" on the ground level. The internal main street activates the central circulation for the headquarters, introducing a small-town scale to the facility. Workplace amenities such as food service, conference and training facilities along with in-house conveniences such as banking, sundry store, museum, beauty salons, dry-cleaning and fitness center, are directly accessed from the interior street, bringing a heightened level of convenience, vitality and interaction into the workplace.

Hansen's team enhanced the new circulating experience by enclosing the internal street within a series of beautiful skylit atria, complete with water features and enticing views to the site's natural splendor: exterior lakes, wetlands, gardens, as well as jogging paths and outdoor sports venues. Informal seating areas were designed within the atrium to encourage impromptu meetings and conversations as well as planned large-scale public events for marketing and community outreach.

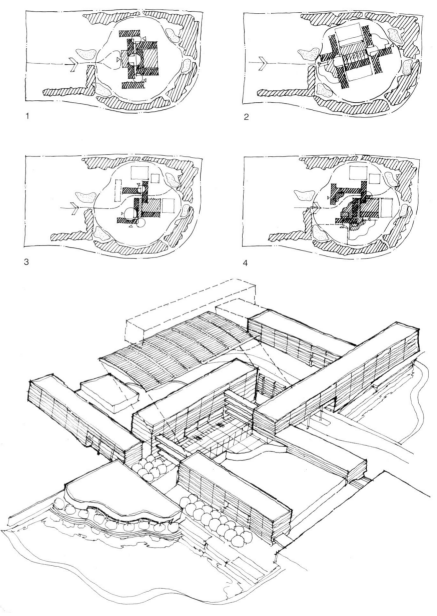

1 Master plan alternative
2 Master plan alternative
3 Final master plan, Phase 1
4 Final master plan, Phase 2

Sears Integrated Business Headquarters

42

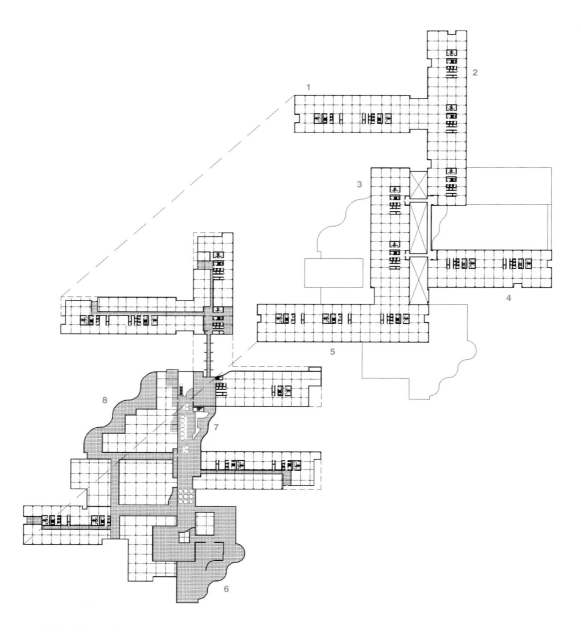

1 Building A (typical floor)
2 Building B (typical floor)
3 Building C (typical floor)
4 Building D (typical floor)
5 Building E (typical floor)
6 Food service (concourse level)
7 Main Street (concourse level)
8 Conference & Training Center

Sears Integrated Business Headquarters

44

Sears Integrated Business Headquarters

Water features and interior landscaping support these activities further with their inherent acoustic properties, masking the sound within the atrium and allowing a sense of privacy and collegiality to occur within this lively space.

Hansen's strategy in creating the massing and exterior envelope for the complex looked to create a friendly, inviting image for Sears. Buildings are clad in reflective glass to mitigate the visual mass of the structure and mirror the wooded surroundings. The design team sited the complex at the lowest point of the 200-acre site, situated adjacent to untouched wetlands, further reducing the overall scale of the building. Hansen's team, working with a group of landscape and botanical experts, restored the site's original prairie landscape, a strategy that not only reduced maintenance costs, but also brought back indigenous wildlife and flora to the community.

Today, a decade later, Sears continues to flourish in its facility. Rick Kotarba, Director of Corporate Services, states, "I can offer some candid observations on the contribution that David's approach and personal commitment to quality work space have had on the achievement of Sears' goals for its headquarters… Early in the process, he was convinced that the idea of synergy through staff interaction could be fostered through architectural design. The resulting facility provided us with the vital and connective atrium, enhanced with staff amenities beyond the project's original vision."

46

Sears Integrated Business Headquarters

Financial Services Headquarters
Riverwoods, Illinois

In 2002, when the Financial Services Company approached David Hansen, it was looking for an architect with large-scale corporate design experience to develop a phased design approach to its existing modernist office building and large suburban site in Riverwoods, Illinois. The company had a specific goal for the project: to consolidate the functions of the existing 1980's building and plan for a new multiphased complex to allow the organization to effectively adapt to growth, consolidation and/or reconfiguration. Because of the company's rapid growth, the project required that the new buildings adopt a sense of connectivity, where information and new knowledge are shared through the interaction of its expanding employee base.

As a first step, Hansen and his team developed a master plan to establish future growth strategies for the entire corporate campus site. An existing retention pond on the site was enlarged and redesigned as a scenic lake for existing and future building sites to utilize as both an amenity and a visual enhancement. The geometry of the master plan is organized along a pedestrian loop around the entire lake with a system of bridges and service tunnels. The first phase of the master plan occupies 468,200 square feet and includes a 386,500-square-foot corporate office building and an 81,700-square-foot employee service pavilion. Hansen and his team master planned the site to allow for a phased expansion that can potentially double in square footage.

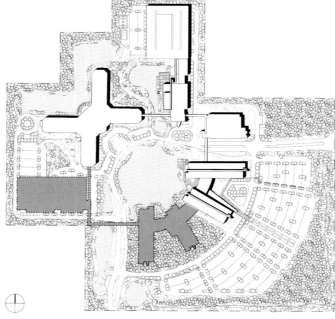

Site plan

The new office building, sited adjacent to the lake, comprises two office wings linked together by a central atrium. From the atrium, a glass-structured canopy articulates the arrival sequence onto the campus. The location of this glass atrium, centered between the two building wings, supports the client's goal for connectivity within the headquarters complex. Here, the atrium functions as an important hub for the organization with a conference and training center along with a "grab and go" coffee bar to act as the intersection and point of connection for staff and visitors throughout the day.

Additional amenities are located adjacent to the headquarters building in the Employee Service Pavilion. Sited to act as a bridge between the original headquarters building and newer buildings, the pavilion is positioned to capitalize on the beautiful views of the site and the adjacent lake. The pavilion supports the organization's broad range of conferencing needs and provides a flexible dining center to accommodate large and small groups plus a fully equipped fitness center. In addition, a series of outdoor dining terraces were designed to take advantage of the pavilions' proximity to the lake as well as jogging and walking paths that offer employees access to the entire wooded site and natural wetlands.

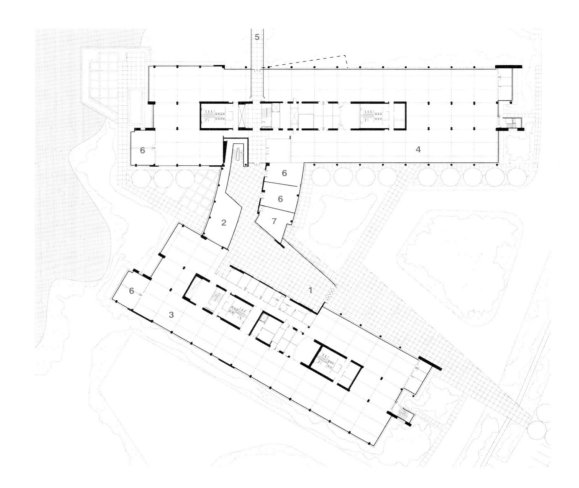

1 Entry lobby
2 Atrium connection
3 Office
4 Office

5 Bridge
6 Conference room
7 Café

Financial Services Headquarters

57

Financial Services Headquarters

To satisfy the client's need for a highly flexible space to accommodate the group's large interrelated departments, Hansen developed a virtually column-free, 40-foot clear span structural system for each building wing. At the outset of the project, the team developed conceptual planning scenarios to establish the optimal dimensions of the standard building module to best facilitate uninhibited future planning strategies.

A central challenge from the client that permeated all aspects of design was to create a visually unified campus without relegating the original headquarters building to a secondary building. Thus, a palette of precast cladding, tinted glazing and metal panels, colored to accent and harmonize with the granite cladding on the original building, was utilized throughout the campus. To create a sense of invitation, as well as enhance views to the outside, non-tinted energy efficient glazing was used at all major entries, circulation routes and public spaces.

A delighted client felt that, "Every aspect of our goals was realized within the interim phase of the project: an integrated and connected campus, a new set of buildings that are aesthetically and functionally of the highest quality, and though still awaiting the third phase, a campus that seems complete and ordered."

Financial Services Headquarters

Financial Services Headquarters

The Reliance Group National Headquarters Building
New Mumbai, India

The Reliance Group (Reliance), a producer of textiles and refined oil products, and India's largest private sector company, holds a place on Fortune's Global 500 list of the world's largest corporations.

In 2002, Reliance decided to relocate its corporate offices from a building in Mumbai, India to a large land holding in New Mumbai. The company turned to David Hansen to create a master plan for the 158-acre site that includes the Perkins+Will designs for the main gateway to the site, a new National Headquarters Building, a Petroleum House Headquarters, a Conference/Training facility, a Bio-Research laboratory and various site amenities.

Initially, the new campus will accommodate 15,000 employees from varying fields to function as the hub of all Reliance activities. The ultimate campus is designed to accommodate more than 30,000 staff members. A lifelong dream of Reliance's late founder, Dhirubhai Ambani, the new campus was brought to life by Mukesh Ambani, the current Chief Executive Officer and Managing Director of the group. Ambani set specific goals for the design of the National Headquarters Building: to communicate the organization's expanding global position, support the young and informal corporate culture that is unique to Reliance, and promote the high value it places on the wellbeing of its employees.

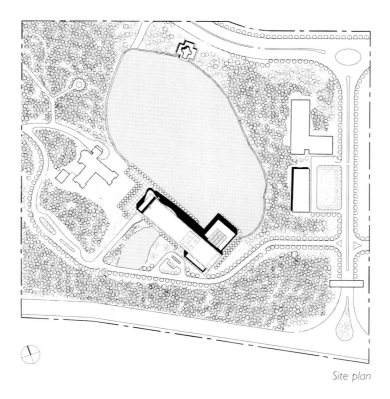

Site plan

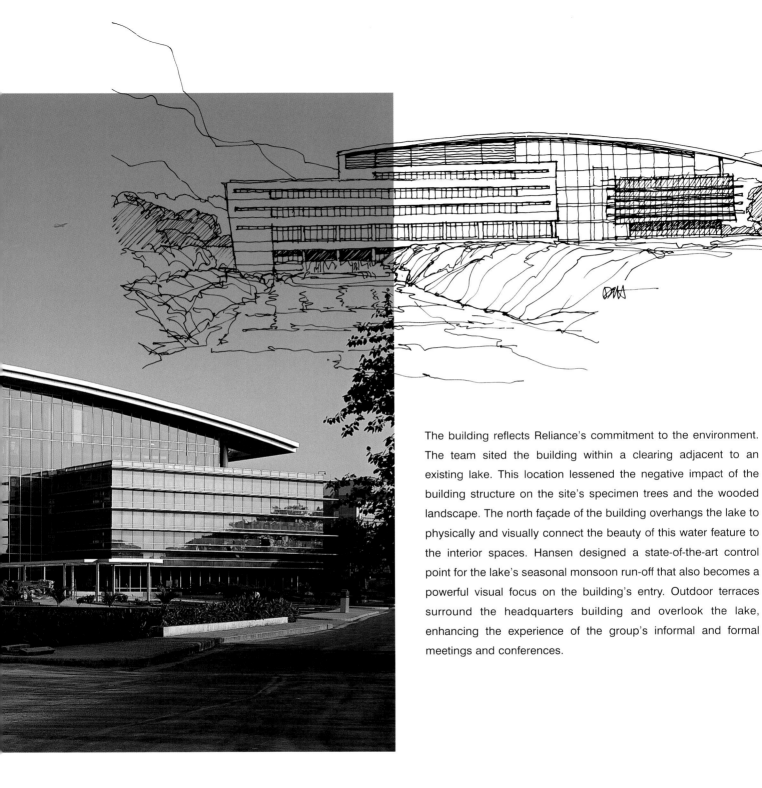

The building reflects Reliance's commitment to the environment. The team sited the building within a clearing adjacent to an existing lake. This location lessened the negative impact of the building structure on the site's specimen trees and the wooded landscape. The north façade of the building overhangs the lake to physically and visually connect the beauty of this water feature to the interior spaces. Hansen designed a state-of-the-art control point for the lake's seasonal monsoon run-off that also becomes a powerful visual focus on the building's entry. Outdoor terraces surround the headquarters building and overlook the lake, enhancing the experience of the group's informal and formal meetings and conferences.

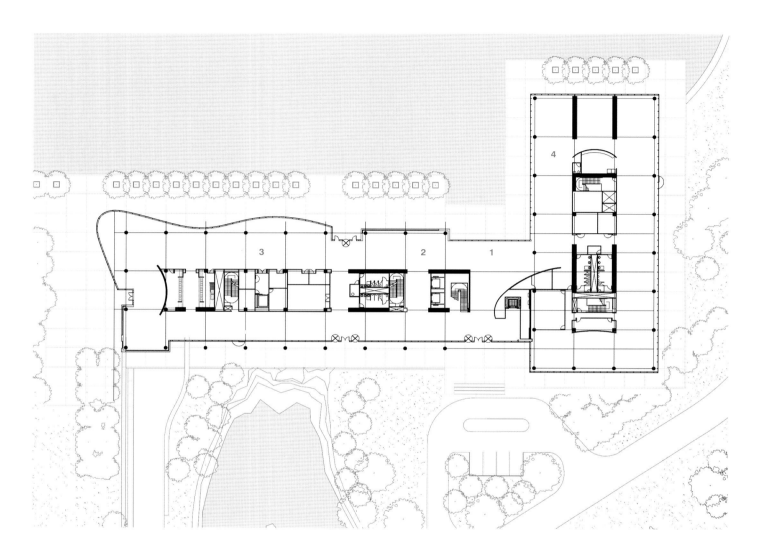

1 Lobby
2 Business center
3 Food service
4 Conference center

The Reliance Group National Headquarters Building

The central five-story atrium activates the central planning concept for the headquarters building by providing an opportunity for interaction among and between departments. This glass atrium, visible from a distance, displays the dynamic energy of Reliance's young, diverse workforce as part of the arrival sequence onto the campus. The three interior bridges span the 18-meter-wide skylit atrium to define the circulation path between the two building wings, connecting workplace activities and dining with the conference and training areas. The location of water elements below the atrium's central stair and the glass-enclosed chairman's elevator allow them to seemingly float within the space. Comfortable seating within the atrium allows staff and visitors to converse as they look to vistas across the lake and glimpse the vitality of business within.

The larger of the two wings houses the offices of Reliance's executive staff and their support personnel as well as the visitors' high-tech business center, multi-use food service areas and meeting/dining rooms. The chairman's wing, the smaller glass pavilion, juts into the lake and allows his office on the top floor to have access to a private terrace and unobstructed views to the lake and the rest of the campus beyond. The lower floors contain staff offices, support and a state-of-the-art conference center at grade, directly adjacent to the lakeside terrace.

Architecturally, the two major masses, and thus their functions, are articulated separately by varying their materials. The chairman's pavilion is clad with reflective glass while the executive wing is clad in French limestone with the fenestration combining horizontal transoms above larger strip windows. The complex is unified by utilizing prominent horizontal sunscreens throughout, the contiguous atrium space between volumes, and by the dramatic curvilinear roof that floats above the composition.

Understanding the importance of the building's impact on the surrounding environment, Hansen's design incorporates a variety of sustainable features. These include: the reuse of an existing historic building, stormwater management systems, use of native plants and water-efficient landscaping, the use of local stone and masonry material, use of certified wood and rapidly renewable products, daylighting, automated lights and temperature control with high efficiency mechanical systems, systems for recyclable materials, and a waste management program.

Harwood International Building Phase 9

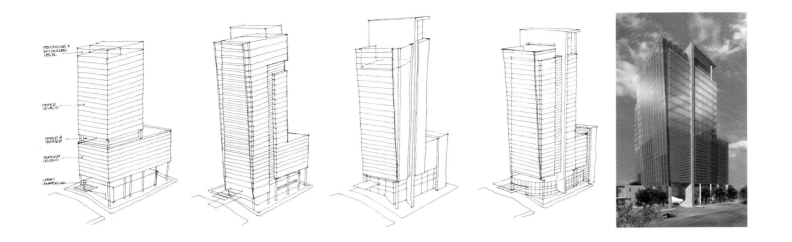

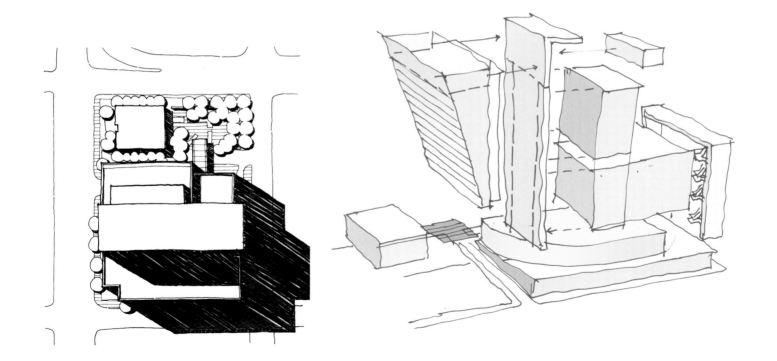

CIRD Nile Gateway Center
Cairo, Egypt

After providing site selection and land acquisition services to the two largest developers and the largest bank in Egypt, CIRD, the resulting entity, hired Hansen to master plan and design its new 71,000-square-meter office and mixed-use complex, located in Giza, just north of Cairo's busy central business district.

The overall parti for the complex utilizes a traditional Islamic courtyard at the heart of the project. This approach provides both a strong cultural tie and a solution for the overwhelming need for natural light and views to the Nile. The initial rectangular solid of the prescribed zoning envelope is divided into two flanking masses to define the center space, increase the perimeter and maximize direct and oblique views to the Nile. A four-story atrium emphasizes the main entry off the Corniche, and also links the north and south building masses.

Proceeding east from the atrium toward the Nile, a visual corridor is established, which sequences a series of terraces in the courtyard, culminating at a gateway near the river's edge. The north mass, to further enhance views to the Nile, shortens in length and extrudes vertically in a curvilinear form, allowing unparalleled views of Cairo. This combination of plan and architectural gestures results in a strong and individual identity—one that provides the highest quality amenities and flexible and productive internal space for its owners and tenants.

94

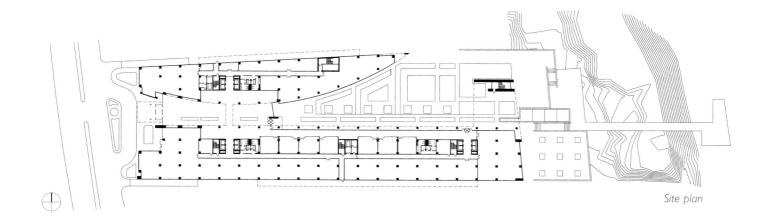

Site plan

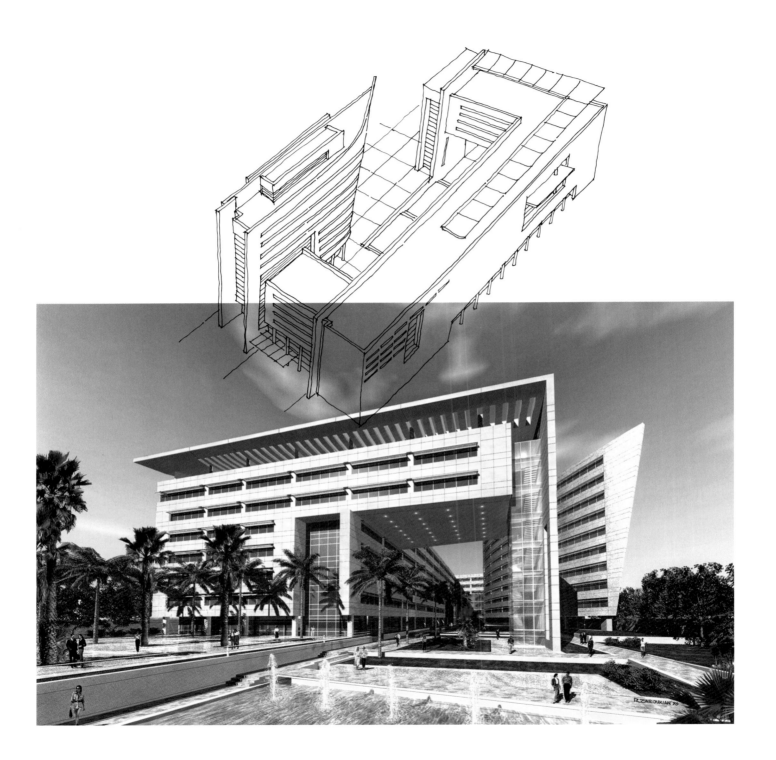

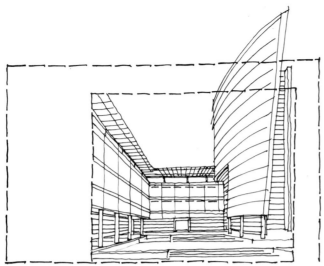

The building is clad in silver-grey granite, with both flamed and polished finishes. The curtain wall is of clear anodized mullions with grey-tinted, high-efficiency glazing. Water-efficient landscape techniques are used for the roof gardens and terrace plantings, which also utilize regional and drought-resistant vegetation.

CIRD Nile Gateway Center

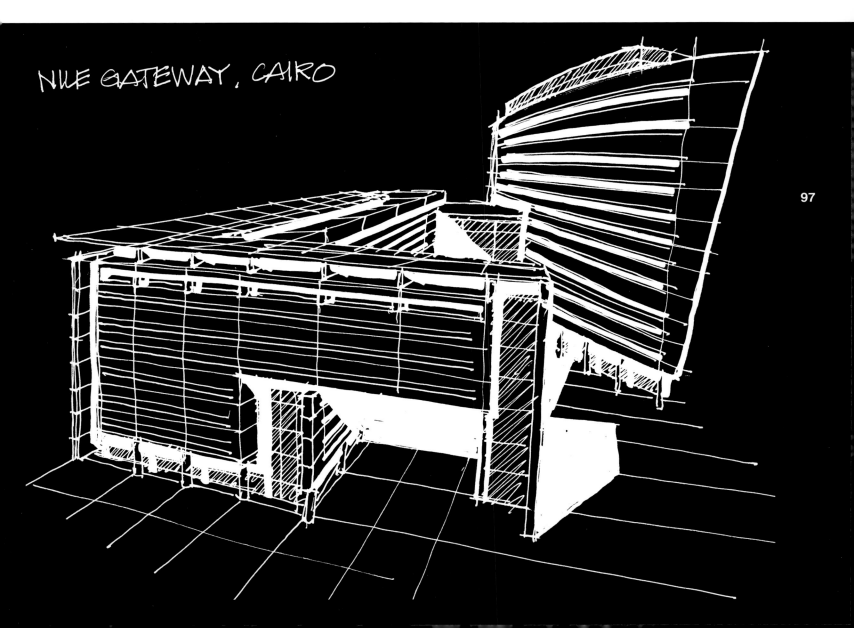

NILE GATEWAY, CAIRO

97

FLOOR PLATES TOO
DEEP NO VIEWS OR
NATURAL LIGHT

BASIC ZONING
VOLUME

CREATE ACCESS TO
NATURAL LIGHT &
COURTYARD-CULTURE

CREATE ACCESS TO
NATURAL LIGHT &
COURTYARD-CULTURE

SHORTEN & EXTEND
TOWER VERTICALLY FOR
IDENTITY & VIEWS

SHAPE END OF TOWER
TO ALLOW COURTYARD
VIEWS OF NILE

CREATE VISUAL
CORRIDOR TO NILE
"GATEWAY"

Samsung Research and Development Headquarters Nexus Centre
Taejon, Korea

Samsung's stated goals for its new Research and Development Headquarters were to create the premier complex of buildings in the emerging Science City of Taejon, Korea, and to develop a signature identity that was commensurate with its international reputation in electronics and communications.

The master plan encompasses the formal organization and integration of more than 240,000 square meters of functions from Samsung's aerospace, heavy industry and chemical divisions as well as linkage from these divisions back and through the headquarters building. Since management and research training regimens require much of the staff to live on the campus for months at a time, an ambitious complex of dormitories, fitness, and recreational facilities is integrated with the training and conferencing facilities, in a more secluded area of the site. A formal boulevard, one of the master plan's organizing elements, originates at the main entry to the south, follows the terrain in a grand sweep and connects with the dormitory and recreation components to the northeast. A secondary system of roadways allows staff and service vehicles to circulate to all buildings and parking areas without accessing the formal boulevard.

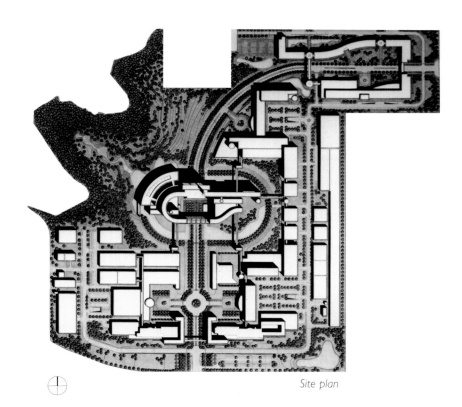

Site plan

The 41,000-square-meter headquarters building is the focal point of the campus and functions as the symbolic town square of a highly unified and collaborative research community and includes the tallest structure in the area. To support this important role, the headquarters building is sited on the mid-point of the boulevard and is the visual terminus of both gateways.

Historic Korean planning theory and culturally significant elements such as a plinth, water moat, formal bridge and honorific town square at the very center of the building, promote the dignity and cultural importance of Samsung's headquarters building to visitors and dignitaries.

A strong and muscular expression of structure, white metal columns and long-span steel trusses, combined with a taut reflective skin creating a highly technical presence, together with traditional materials of local woods and stone, help promote a warm and regionally sensitive interior environment.

100

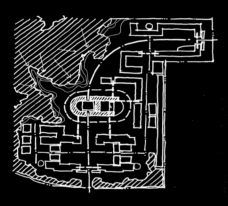 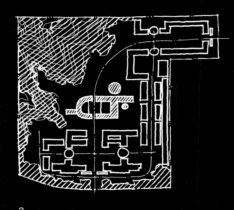 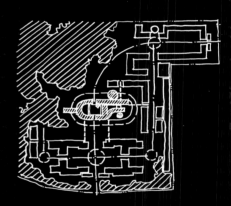

1   2   3

1 Master plan phase option
2 Master plan phase option
3 Final master plan

Samsung Research and Development Headquarters Nexus Centre

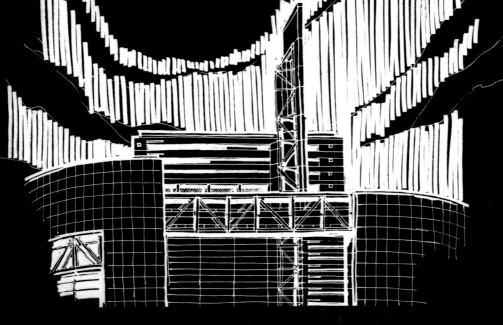

World Trade Center

Beijing, China

The World Trade Center challenged Hansen and his team to combine an expansive 520,000-square-meter mixed-use program on a four-block site into a unified and comprehensive force for that area of Beijing's emerging central business district.

With Perkins+Will acting as master architect and planner, a comprehensive team of architects and planners was assembled with specialists in the various functional types, including Altoon + Porter, SWA, and WATC.

Existing city circulation patterns, neighboring uses, and view corridors are among the parameters distilled into the design to create a harmonious and vibrant external public space that acts as the focal point for the entire project.

Site plan

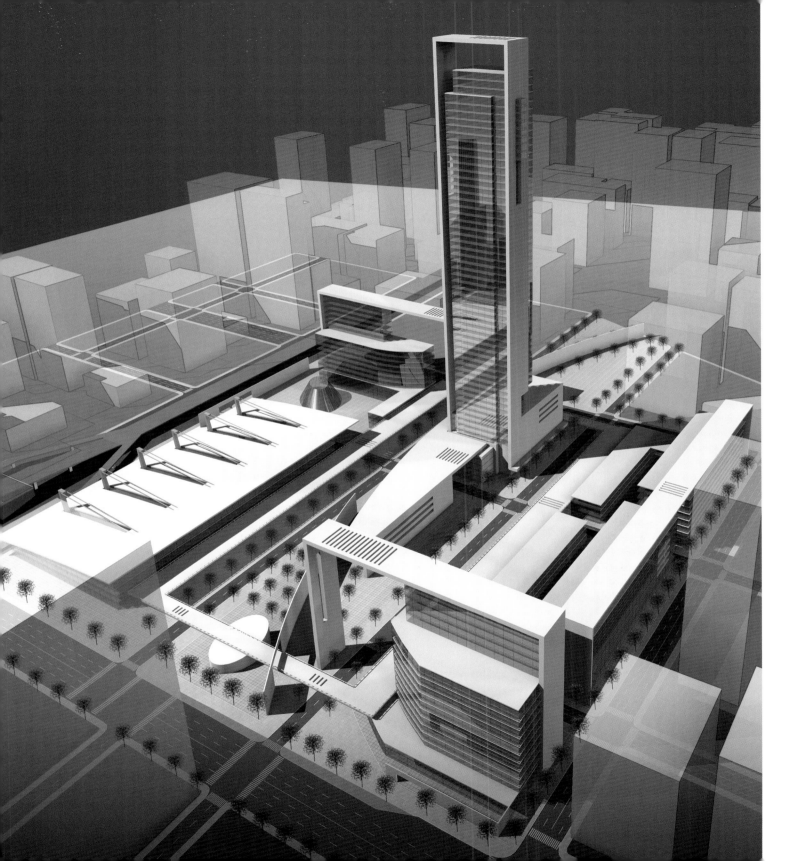

Placement and synergies of the functional elements act to define and punctuate space. Major elements such as the office tower, retail and office blocks, hotels, the convention center and conference center are sensitively placed and interrelated to develop a defined and unified plan. Thus, the central high-rise office tower is placed at the terminus of two external north–south garden areas, allowing unbroken visual and pedestrian access from the city beyond. The location of the office tower and hotel elements exploit their height and architectural tectonics to provide identity and compositional harmony. The convention center and lower office and retail blocks add enclosure, vitality and definition to the ensemble, and create urban-scale gateways.

The design provides a separate identity to each functional element yet portrays an overall architectural context and unifying theme.

104

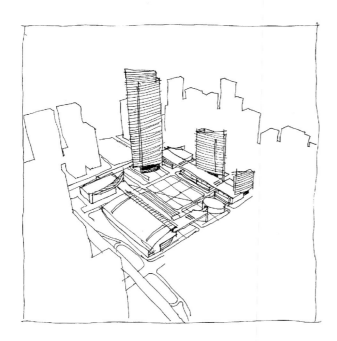

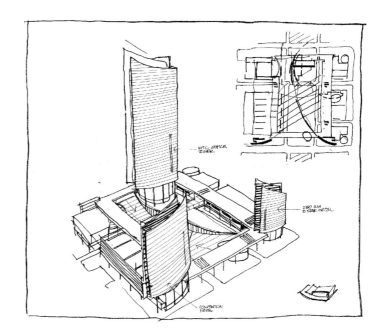

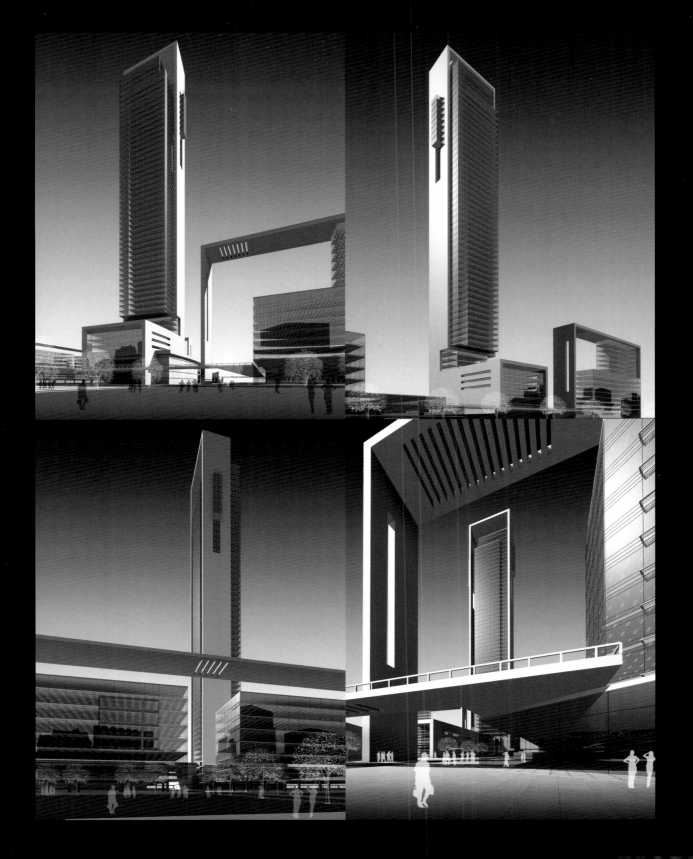

World Trade Center

Corporate index

05
2005
Shimao Pudong Mixed-use Development
Shanghai, China
3,700,000 sq ft (343,741 sq m)
Master plan, architecture, interiors

05
2005
New Hotel Development
Austin, Texas
368,480 sq ft (34,233 sq m)
Master plan, architecture, interiors

110

04
2004
World Trade Center
Beijing, China
5,597,233 sq ft (520,000 sq m)
Master plan, architecture

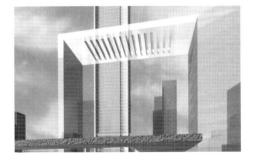

04
2004
5th Square Beijing
Beijing, China
1,000,000 sq ft (92,903 sq m)
Architecture (concept and schematic design)

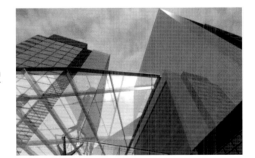

New Mumbai, India · **Reliance Convention & Learning Center**

344,445 sq ft (32,000 sq m)

Master plan, architecture, interiors

Chicago, Illinois, USA · **American Red Cross Headquarters**

57,450 sq ft (5,346 sq m)

Architecture, interiors

02
2002

Northfield, Illinois, USA · **Kraft Headquarters Expansion**

220,000 sq ft (20,439 sq m)

Architecture, interiors

02
2002

Dallas, Texas, USA · **Harwood International Phase IX**

490,000 sq ft (45,522 sq m)

Master plan, architecture

02
2002

02   **Petroleum House Headquarters**   New Mumbai, India

2002   275,000 sq ft (25,548 sq m)

Master plan, architecture, interiors

01   **Shindome Tower**   Tokyo, Japan

2001   1,300,000 sq ft (120,774 sq m)

Architecture in association with Ysui Architects, Tokyo

112

01   **The Reliance Group National Headquarters**   New Mumbai, India

2001   172,222 sq ft (16,000 sq m)

Master plan, architecture, interiors

01   **Eden Shores**   Haywood, California, USA

2001   200,000 sq ft (18,580 sq m)

Master plan, architecture

Riverwoods, Illinois, USA   **Financial Services Headquarters**   **01**

Office Building   2001

386,500 sq ft (35,907 sq m)

Master plan, architecture, interiors

Riverwoods, Illinois, USA   **Financial Services Headquarters**   **01**

Employee Service Pavilion   2001

81,700 sq ft (7,590 sq m)

Master plan, architecture, interiors

113

Tokyo, Japan   **Mori Trust at Tokyo Station**   **99**

1,720,000 sq ft (159,793 sq m)   1999

Architecture in association with Ysui Architects, Tokyo

Columbus, Ohio, USA   **Bank One Expansion**   **98**

1,200,000 sq ft (111,484 sq m)   1998

Architecture, interiors

98
1998

Pyramid Heights   Giza, Egypt

1,180,000 sq ft (109,626 sq m)
Master plan, architecture

98
1998

CIRD   Cairo, Egypt

764,238 sq ft (71,000 sq m)
Master plan, architecture

114

97
1997

Sears Integrated Business Group   Hoffman Estates, Illinois, USA
Headquarters Expansion

500,000 sq ft (46,451 sq m)
Architecture, interiors

97
1997

Abu Dhabi National Oil Company   Abu Dhabi, UAE

600,000 sq ft (55,742 sq m)
Master plan, architecture

Lake Forest, Illinois, USA · **W.W. Grainger Inc. Headquarters** · 97
800,000 sq ft (74,322 sq m) · 1997
Master plan, architecture, interiors

Taejon, Korea · **Samsung Corporation Headquarters** · 96
2,615,630 sq ft (243,000 sq m) · 1996
Master plan, architecture, interiors

115

Elgin, Illinois, USA · **Motorola Offices and Manufacturing** · 96
525,000 sq ft (48,774 sq m) · 1996
Master plan, architecture, interiors

Columbus, Ohio, USA · **Bank One Corporate Center** · 94
880,000 sq ft (81,755 sq m) · 1994
Master plan, architecture, interiors

93
1993

NBD Bank Corporate Center, Phase One Farmington Hills, Illinois, USA

710,000 sq ft (65,961 sq m)

Master plan, architecture, interiors

92
1992

Singapore Science Park Gateway Building Singapore

220,000 sq ft (20,439 sq m)

Master plan, architecture

116

92
1992

Singapore Science Park Amenity Center Singapore

50,000 sq ft (4,645 sq m)

Architecture

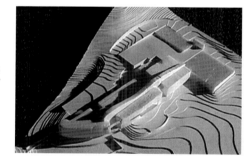

91
1991

Sam Yang Company Headquarters Taejon, Korea

372,431 sq ft (34,600 sq m)

Master plan, architecture

Oakbrook, Illinois, USA   **Edge Systems Inc. Headquarters**   **91**

110,000 sq ft (10,219 sq m)   1991

Master plan, architecture

Carmel, Indiana, USA   **Thompson Consumer Electronics**   **90**

350,000 sq ft (32,516 sq m)   1990

Master plan, architecture, interiors

117

Des Plaines, Illinois, USA   **Wheels Inc. Headquarters Expansion**   **89**

60,000 sq ft (5,574 sq m)   1989

Master plan, architecture, interiors

Hoffman Estates, Illinois, USA   **Sears Integrated Business Group**   **89**

1,900,000 sq ft (176,516 sq m)   1989

Master plan, architecture, interiors

88
1988

Toyota Regional Headquarters   Aurora, Illinois, USA

2,500,000 sq ft (232,258 sq m)

Master plan, architecture

87
1987

Abbot Laboratories   Chicago, Illinois, USA

400,000 sq ft (37,161 sq m)

Architecture, master plan

86
1986

Kraft Headquarters   Northfield, Illinois, USA

505,000 sq ft (46,916 sq m)

Master plan, architecture, interiors

The work listed in this timeline represents David Hansen's comprehensive experience in corporate architecture. These projects encompass master planning, built architecture and interiors as well as design competitions.

Acknowledgments

David Hansen is sincerely grateful for the contributions of the following individuals:

Fred Afshari
James Allen
Chuck Anderson
Todd Baisch
Robert Barnes
Franco Barsi
Curt Behnke
Nathalie Belanger
Wally Bissonnette
John Bower
Geoff Brooksher
David Brubaker
Cindy Coleman
Ray Coleman
Robert Cooke
Malaika Corsentina
Kim Creswell
Paul deSantis
Yang Ding
Bill Doerge
Neil Frankel
Gordon Gilmore
Randy Guillot
Don Haan
Walt Heffernan
Mike Henthorn
Peggy Hoffman
Jin Huh
Bonnie Humphrey
John Jackowski
Shelly Jensen
Marty Jurasek
Sheryl Kanter
Carl Knutson
Keith Kreinik

Pauline Kurtides
David Larsen
Joe Lesch
Jim Lubawy
Mike McPhail
Milan Miladinovich
Gokul Natarajan
Hans Neumann
Gutman Nimrod
Rod Noble
Jon Nunemaker
June Oh
John O'Neil
Terrence Owens
Frank Pettinati
Paula Pilola
David Powell
Elisabeth Quebe
Louis Raia
Carol Reeser
Rick Reindel
Bill Schmalz
Nick Seierup
Waleed Shalalan
Len Skiba
Eric Spielman
Judd Storey
Hans Thummel
Maria Tiling-Lewis
Raymond Tsai
Michael Weiner
Serena Wen
Gary Wheeler
Phil Zinni

Special thanks to Shelly Jensen and Paul deSantis for their unwavering enthusiasm, collaboration and support.

Photography credits